Only A Soldier Understands

Every GI's Reflections and
Reminiscences of Military Life

Clay Lifto

outskirtspress
DENVER, COLORADO

Table of Contents

Preface

To my brothers and sisters in the service.

This book is dedicated to you ... to the millions of men and women who have worn the American uniform in the Army, the Navy, the Air Force, the Marines, and the Coast Guard, whether on active duty or in the Guards or Reserves. Your commitment to service on behalf of freedom everywhere is a worthy quest, no matter where you are from or what your background has been.

May each of you indeed find the adventure you are seeking, the fulfillment that your sacrifice will bring to you, and the life that is truly worth living. May these pages help each of us to understand the truth about ourselves more clearly, and may each of us have the *courage* to make right decisions in life and the *power* to act on them.

About the Author

Clay Lifto retired as an SFC from twenty-eight years of service in the Army and Army Reserves. He served in 1968-1969 in Vietnam, as well as tours in Turkey, Germany, Washington, Texas, and California. He earned twenty-three military decorations and completed over a dozen military courses and schools as honor graduate, including the Defense Language Institute (three times) and several electronic warfare schools. In 2000 he was awarded the Medal of Peace by the Russian-Ukrainian Afghanistan War Veterans Association for his humanitarian efforts in eastern Ukraine (1991-2000).

He is now Professor Emeritus of Management at Kirkwood Community College in Cedar Rapids, Iowa, where he has taught for over twenty-nine years. During that time he has acted as a consultant to Ford Aerospace and has provided critiques for INSCOM's C3 exercises. At Kirkwood he was selected twice for *Who's Who in Education*, and he was chosen by the National Institute for Staff and Organizational Development as one of the nation's Top Ten Picks of 1996.

Clay is also a pastor and church planter, working with five churches in Ukraine and retiring as pastor from a new church in Lisbon, Iowa. He has completed a master's degree in Christian education and a doctorate in ministries (pastoral leadership). He and his wife Ruth have two children – Nickie, who works in the Fayetteville, North Carolina area as a counselor for families with young children with disabilities; and Christopher, who is an Army helicopter pilot stationed in Afghanistan.

Acknowledgments

Thank you men and women of the Armed Forces, for allowing me to share these reflections and reminiscences with you. Despite the many years that have passed by since I left the Army and Army Reserves, there will always be that undeniable connection between us in the military family. And my belief is that the heart I share with you in these pages has grown significantly because of the input of people like you, who live a life of significance.

Thank you specifically to my good GI friends Randy Geneske, and Pastors Phil Foster and Nick Rich, each of whom was able to critique my writing with a unique perspective.

Thanks also to those many unnamed people in my life who have made it more interesting. Likely, left on my own, I'd be living in a jail cell today! But thanks to the input of people who loved me despite my faults, my life has become truly worth living.

And thanks to my mom, Mattie Ginapp, who made a decision about God while she was a young adult, and passed it on to me. Her unfailing and sacrificially generous love for me her son, and for so many others who have been fortunate to encounter her during her long and productive life, has been an inspiration to know Him also.

And thanks to my son Chris, whose decision to join the Army, and Kjerstin's willingness to accompany him on the adventure, has been a confirmation to me that I made the right choice many years before.

In a much different way, I give a hug to my daughter Nickie, whose insights point me to things that are much more important in life than my personal ego and accomplishing life goals.

Thanks also to my son-in-law Tony Gael and my sister Rose Kendall, whose aspirations to write about what they know eliminated my excuses not to.

And thanks to my wife of forty-two years, Ruth, whose indefatigable love and devotion to this unworthy soldier, has been the greatest gift that I could possibly receive on this earth. It is said that a true test of a loving wife is having the patience for her husband to grow up. May I live long enough for her to enjoy the fruits of her patience!

How to Read This Book

Each short vignette encapsulates something about military life. It's written as a story, from the days of the recruiter to the end of a career – if you stay with me that long. My hope is that as I tell my story, each of you is able to reflect on your own, and maybe even share it with others.

In fact, you might want to get together with comrades and go through each one with them. You'd likely share some great times together as you tell your stories and laugh together about your experiences!

I found that the writing of this book has been a great catharsis for me. I myself had some difficult memories of Vietnam that I've had to deal with, some of which took some counseling with other old-time vets. For some of you, most of your life is still ahead of you. And these pages may provide you with some wisdom from those that have traveled the road ahead of you. My advice? Travel through the pages of this book with someone else who wears the uniform.

And for my heroes, leaders who commit themselves to the lives of others, I am asking you to round up the troops on a Sunday afternoon or evening, buy the junk food and pop, and share each other's stories and camaraderie. May each of us then gain the courage to seek the truth about ourselves and our place in this world, so that we may one day meet God face to face with a smile.

Let's get started!

1

Escaping, Once Again

And I thought that running off to college to escape from Dad's tough discipline would solve all my problems! So here I was, flunking out. All my money – gone. For two months now I hadn't been able to get out of bed on time to get to my 8:00 a.m. class. I was taking long walks away from campus so that no one would spot me. Mom would find out pretty soon, though. Of that I was sure.

But for now I just couldn't make it on my own. And, in my humiliation I couldn't face *them*. I had been so cocky. I was going to show *them* that I didn't need any of *them*. And now I was desperate. I was broke. The college dumped me from my part-time janitorial job, oddly enough because I usually didn't show up, and even then I didn't get all the cleaning done. What was going to happen to me?

Maybe Dad was right about me. I *was* worthless. I *would* turn out to be nothing but a bum. I grew up with a chip on my shoulder. I was bitter about my rough treatment as a kid. All I wanted to do was get away from home, get away from my parents, and get away from all the yelling and accusing that went on every single day.

Maybe I was an escapist. I had run away from home once a few years prior, to get away from another whipping. I knew I deserved it. I broke out all the windows in the chicken coop! Oh, but it was so much fun – hurling those corn cobs – to smash through the shattering glass!

It seems like I ran away from all my problems. First, I'd avoid them – especially homework, even through my more adult years. It's possible that I could have handled going to class in college, if the first class hadn't been so early in the morning. But the homework. You had to read stuff. And then write stuff. And there were so many more interesting things to do with my life.

Man, that recruiter at the mall looked cool in his uniform! All those scars. And all those medals – he looked like he'd been through some tough battles. And what a nice guy! It seemed as though he liked me just fine. He smiled when I came in. He even shook my hand and patted me on the back!

1. What was your situation just before you decided to join the military?

2. Why do you suppose that *escaping* from home is such an issue with teenagers in America?

3. When someone is in a tough situation like flunking out of college, what are other ways to get out of the jam?

A Note from the Commander.

And not many days later, the younger son gathered everything together and went on a journey into a distant country, and there he squandered his estate with loose living. Now when he had spent everything, a severe famine occurred in that country and he began to be impoverished. (Luke 15:13-14 NASB)

2
The Recruiter

He was wearing his dress greens the day that I met him. He was a Korean War veteran with ribbons completely burying the left side of his chest. Yellow hash marks covered his sleeve from his wrist nearly to where his sergeant's stripes began. I could only stare at what was obviously an all-American hero.

When he glanced my way at the recruiting station, I must have looked pretty stupid, standing there staring. But he only smiled and invited me over to chat. He put his hand on my shoulder, and made me feel as though I could actually become a part of his incredible world.

It was as though every question I could ask about life, he already knew. He understood my frustrations with life. He understood how I just needed to get away – away from school, away from my parents, away from being a failure. He understood my need for a new beginning. He understood that I couldn't make it on my own, even though I didn't tell him. And he accepted me as I was.

I thought Army sergeants were supposed to be mean guys! This guy could tell me my own story. And despite my weaknesses, he had an important job for me. He would get me trained and ready to perform, even though I had already dropped out of school. Isn't the Army remarkable?

Was the Army really the answer to my problems, or was I *really* gullible? I didn't know for sure, but it seemed to me like the solution I needed.

1. Why do you suppose that recruiters are able to establish such a rapport with a recruit?

2. Why was I so willing to get sucked in by the Army recruiter?

3. Whom do you know, that could really use a friend right now? Are your skills as sharp as the recruiters' at making friends?

Note from the Commander.
I have called you friends, for all things that I have heard from My Father I have made known to you. (John 15:14b NASB)

3

Armed Forces Entrance and Examination Station[1]

The Armed Forces Entrance and Examination Station, Minneapolis, Minnesota – was a scary place! I'm a small-town farm boy, and wandering around the big city was an adrenalin rush! Huge buildings that crack your neck, traffic lanes only an athlete could negotiate, and downtown noises that would keep the hens from ever laying another egg!

I was ready for the tests. I even went to bed early the previous night, around 9:00, just to make sure I wouldn't be tired. I knew I was pretty smart, but this was going to be my chance to get somewhere in life (again), and I didn't want to blow it (this time).

I got up early that Monday morning. The recruiter pulled up outside at 7:00, just like he said he would. It was mighty nice of him to be willing to drive me into town for the testing. He even offered to get me a donut and some coffee when we checked in at the AFEES.

---

[1] Yes, I know. It's no longer called AFEES. In fact, that's now more like the abbreviation for the PX system, isn't it? It changed long ago to MEPS. But do you know what the MEPS initials stand for?

Wow, the building was huge--people scurrying everywhere. I'd have been lost in a minute if it weren't for the sarge keeping his eye on me. What is it about big stuff – big mountains, big buildings, big stuff – that really gets a guy going? Something about the whole atmosphere got me pumped. It's like some-one hooked one end of a jumper cable to my eyelids. I felt as though this was the beginning of something *really* big in my life. I couldn't wait to hear the results.

It would be a week or so, and then I'd have to go down there again to get the results of the tests and also get a physical. It would be hard to sleep while I waited. I wasn't going to class any-more, and Mom and Dad still didn't know anything about this.

1. When have you ever set foot in a world *bigger* than you had ever experienced before?

2. Was there ever a point in your life where you felt as though you were on the edge of a great opportunity ready to happen?

3. Do you suppose that there is a *relationship* between "doing life the right way" and attaining a fulfilling or exciting life?

Note from the Commander.
I came that they may have life and have it abundantly. (John 10:10 NASB)

For I know the plans I have for you," declares the Lord, "plans to prosper you and not to harm you, plans to give you hope and a future. (Jeremiah 29:11 NIV)

4

Chosen

"Mr. Lifto, come with me." Sergeant Gruff glared down at me, as I waited for the results of the test battery.

The recruiter warned me about the long day I would endure in preparation for entering the Army. I hadn't selected any particular school yet, because I didn't know what I would qualify for or what was going to be open.

The Vietnam War was really gearing up that spring of 1965, so I wanted to make sure that I didn't wind up in the infantry as cannon fodder. All I wanted was a good school, so I could get a decent job when I was done. A nice Army post somewhere would be cool, too ... somewhere that I wouldn't have to live in a tent and eat dirt all day long.

So, where was he taking me? What did I do wrong? (Why did I always feel *guilty* when someone called my name?) He whisked me quickly down a long hallway, into a large office area, filled with desks, paperwork, and clacking typewriters, and to the door of a back room where he rapped loudly.

A young thirty-something guy in a dark suit welcomed me in and asked me to sit down. "Do you have a police record? Have you ever done drugs? Do you have any relatives or close friends that live in another country?" I was horrified! What had I done wrong? Was it the test battery? Did I turn out to be a crazed serial murderer?

"No" was my answer to each of the questions. But I was sweating.

"Are you interested in learning a foreign language, like Russian? Have you ever heard of the Army Security Agency? Are you able to keep secrets, even from your family if you need to?" Sure, I could keep secrets from my family! Otherwise I'd likely be in prison!

And within ten minutes, I was signed up for four years instead of three, and I was convinced that the Army was going to turn me into a full-fledged spy!

1. When has anyone ever treated you like you were somebody *special*?

2. Was there an occasion in which you thought maybe you were in trouble, but it turned out that you were getting praised for something instead? Do you suppose someone can have a guilt complex, and just feel guilty any time there is any excitement?

3. Describe a time when you felt as though you were *chosen* for something really important, as though all your life was just a preparation for this moment.

Note from the Commander.

Before I formed you in the womb I knew you, before you were born I set you apart. (Jeremiah 1:5a NIV)

5
The Physical

It had been a few years since my last high school physical. Even then the only reason I got one was because it was required for physical education (or Phys Ed or PE or whatever they call it today). But I supposed I could use another one by now – a nice benefit just for joining up with the Army.

Filling out the paperwork was nothing new. They needed to know about my rheumatic fever I endured in 8th grade. I wondered whether the slight heart murmur would ruin this dream for me. But the doctor back then okayed me for athletics in high school, so it shouldn't be a hindrance now, should it? Besides, didn't they need everyone they could get ... because of the war in Vietnam?

Where was the doctor's office? We were all stuck in lines out in a huge, cavernous room! This would take us forever, if we had to go one at a time into the examining room for the humiliating routine of personal inspection. So, where was the doctor's office?

I didn't really look forward to this experience anyway, because I had a pretty dismal view of my body. Sure I was pretty healthy, I thought. I could run all day and not get tired. Country life had been good to me. On the other hand, back on the farm we bathed only once a week, and my body had a lot of zits, which modern medicine didn't figure out until decades later. And I was pretty skinny, with my rib cage popping out in unsightly places. I didn't like the idea of undressing in front of anyone, let alone the doctor. Where was the doctor's office?

"Okay, men, line up over here! Take off all your clothes, hold them in your arms, face the wall, and bend over!"

1. Were you surprised when you had to take your first military physical?

2. What is it that is so humiliating about standing naked among your peers for an Army physical?

3. Why is it that we have such an aversion to public humiliation, even if it tells only the truth about us?

Note from the Commander.

For the word of God is living and active and sharper than a two-edged sword, and piercing as far as the division of soul and spirit, of both joints and marrow, and able to judge the thoughts and intentions of the heart. And there is no creature hidden from His sight, but all things are open and laid bare to the eyes of Him with whom we have to do. (Hebrews 4:12-13 NASB)

6
Breaking the News to My Family

So, that settled it. I was signed up for a four-year hitch, beginning the following week, April 5th, 1965. They would send me to Fort Leonard Wood, Missouri for basic training, and then on to Monterey, California to learn to speak Russian.

The problem was that I hadn't told my parents yet! At first I didn't want to say anything about dropping out of school until I had something *good* to replace it with. After that, I was afraid they would try to scream and shout me right out of the idea. So, I wanted to wait until the deal was set.

Why was I so afraid? It was my life. I could make my own decisions. But I was only eighteen years old. My parents were dictators! They made all the decisions for my life, and berated and belittled me for the few stupid ones that I made on my own. So, of course, this would be another one.

I gave myself the weekend to take the sixty-mile bus trip home from Minneapolis to Red Wing to break the news. It would give them only a few days' notice; and if they did go berserk, I'd be out of there pretty quickly.

So, let's skip right to it. Mom was heartbroken. She had her mind set on me going to college and being some kind of *godly* man. And now I was going to join the ranks of guys who cussed and drank beer and cavorted with strange foreign women. Dad didn't seem to mind, as long as he didn't have to send money. My five brothers and sisters – well, they seemed like a blur at the time. Well, okay. No big deal. Tuesday I could take the bus directly to Minneapolis with my bag packed, and get out of there.

1. How did your family take the news when you told them about joining the military?

2. Why can it be so fearful telling your parents about a decision like this?

3. Once it (telling the news) was over, was it hard to leave home?

Note from the Commander.
But the angel said to them, "Do not be afraid; for behold I bring you good news of great joy which will be for all the people." (Luke 2:10 NASB)

7

The Train Station

A bus trip from home to St. Paul, then to Minneapolis. Then the city bus to the AFEES building once more. Before I even arrived at the AFEES building they had assigned our group a leader. They gave him a voucher for lunch across the street. I don't remember the meal much. It seemed kind of special at the time, though…the idea of eating at a restaurant, and someone else footing the bill. Would wonders never cease!

I was so afraid to leave the group for any reason! Just when I'd enter the bathroom, I was sure the group would head off down the street! I kept my eye on the leader, who seemed rather mature for an Army recruit. Anywhere he went, I followed. Maybe this was good preparation for what was to follow in basic training.

But my fear was of getting lost. We were in the big city, and anything that could go wrong with this adventure was sure to happen to me. All my short life so far, my dad emphasized what a screw-up I was. Actually he used a lot of other words I'd learn to repeat later in basic training. But he used plenty of vocabulary on me. So, I was plenty scared of messing up on this trip.

We were scheduled to take the train late that afternoon, so we had a little time to kill. But there wasn't a meal on the train ride, which would take most of the night with all the stops. It would be the wee hours of the morning when we arrived at some small town in Missouri, after which we still had to take a bus to Ft. Leonard Wood. This was going to be a long trip!

Finally, at the Minneapolis train station, we climbed aboard, and I stowed my suitcase that I'd been lugging around all day. I didn't have much in it other than two changes of clothes and underwear and a shaving kit. But if I ever got any free time off post, I would need whatever I brought along.

This was a modern train?! Our car was nothing more than a row of bunks mounted to both walls, with curtains to pull closed for privacy! This could be a long trip.

1. What was your departure day like when you headed for basic training? Any buses or trains? What kinds of anxieties did you face as you got ready for departure?

2. How *dependent* have you ever felt on following a leader that was assigned to you?

Note from the Commander.

Be anxious for nothing, but in everything by prayer and supplication with thanksgiving let your requests be made known to God. And the peace of God, which surpasses all [k]comprehension, will guard your hearts and your minds in Christ Jesus. (Philippians 4:6-7 NASB)

8

The Train Ride to Fort Leonard Wood

Would they *never* settle down?! Drinking stupidly, shouting incessantly, and even vomiting grotesquely in the train, hour after hour, through the entire night en route to Missouri. Did they not know how we would be greeted upon our arrival at boot camp? Didn't they know we had to show up well-rested and wide awake? What was the matter with these people?

Maybe they were celebrating their last night of freedom. Maybe they were just away from their parents' rule for the first time. Maybe they just wanted to be accepted by the other drunks. Maybe this was the first time they had found someone old enough to buy their booze for them. I didn't know. But I did know that I attempted to shield myself in my top bunk behind the curtain to the maximum extent possible.

And suddenly we arrived … somewhere in Missouri, where we needed to board a commercial bus to Ft. Leonard Wood. It was already around 5:00 a.m. The night was gone. I was starving. Most of the drunks could barely comprehend the daylight, let alone negotiate the few steps to the bus. They were due for a pretty rude awakening in a few hours. At least these last few hours were going to be pretty quiet.

In fact, the passage was as quiet as a sneak attack. As we approached the front gate, no one spoke a word. The doom that awaited us was ominous. In a few moments the receiving area for new recruits came into view. Wow! It looked like there was a welcoming party!

1. How did you spend your last night before basic training began?

2. Were you at all aware of what would be expected of you upon your day of arrival?

3. Have you ever had a time in your life that you spent recklessly, only to later have to face the day of reckoning?

Note from the Commander.

And I will say to my soul, "Soul, you have many goods laid up for many years to come; take your ease, eat, drink and be merry." But God said to him, "You fool! This very night your soul is required of you." (Luke 12:19-20 NASB)

9

The Reception Center

Ahhh, here we are! We pulled in right at suppertime, at the Reception Center, Ft. Leonard Wood, Missouri. A little supper, a hot shower, a long night's sleep, and I'd be fine!

"Get in line, Soldier!"

"Not fast enough! Drop down and give me twenty!"

"Eyes straight forward! Heels together! Toes spread! Chest out! Fingers curled on the seam! You call yourself a soldier!?"

"Double-time!"

"Who you looking at?"

"Five minutes for lunch – that's long enough! Get out of my mess hall!"

What's wrong with these guys?! Why is everybody yelling in my face? When do I get a break? Why do we have to run everywhere? What's with all the pushups? If this is just the Reception Center, what will the *real* basic training be like?!

Hey, wait a minute here! What's with the toilets all lined up and out in the open like this? And the showers are too close together! Where are the cupboards and shelves by the sink to store my stuff? What's with the cement floors? Don't they even have tiling ... or linoleum?

This is my closet? A fourteen-inch-wide, six-foot-tall, green coffin, set up on end? That's it? Where do I put the rest of my clothes? Oh, the foot locker, I suppose. Boy, this floor is shiny (I'll have to remember to *tip* the custodian)!

The bunk isn't bad, though. And I'm used to sharing a bedroom with my three brothers anyway. Maybe a small area carpet and some small plants and an end table, and I'll be fine.

1. What *surprises* were waiting for you, when you were *received* into basic training camp?

2. Did your recruiter offer you the information you needed about basic training up front, or did you find out about it a different way?

3. Why do you suppose that *honesty* up front is a better idea for recruiting good soldiers?

Note from the Commander.

For which one of you, when he wants to build a tower, does not first sit down and calculate the cost to see if he has enough to complete it? Otherwise, when he has laid a foundation and is not able to finish, all who observe it begin to ridicule him. (Luke 14:28-29 NASB)

10
First KP Duty

"Seventh Platoon, line up on the Red Line! Eight Platoon, line up on the Green Line! Ninth Platoon, line up on the Yellow Line!"

And on it went! It was the line-up for breakfast and in-processing. Which platoon was I in? Which color did he say for us? I was all confused! Better stay with the gang from my barracks!

"Any ASA-ers here? I need some smart men in here to help me out!"

I had been recruited to the Army Security Agency. Was that what he was referring to? Maybe he needed help with calculating his supply needs. Or maybe he had an organization issue he couldn't figure out. I raised my hand. Finally my intelligence would pay off. Maybe they'd give me a medal for whatever problem they needed solved.

Tricked! A ruse! I was stuck scraping dirty plates for the next two hours! And nobody seemed to care that I was being abused like that. Were there no dishwashing machines in the Army? Didn't they have better tools than what they gave me?

And why did I have to wear a bag on my head? I felt like one of the Three Stooges! The mess sergeant knew that I was a four-year recruit and had more time to serve than the draftees, so they were free to use me for slave labor as long as they wanted! At least, that's the way I felt about it.

Now, how was I supposed to find my barracks again? They were all green, two-story, wooden, coal-fired barracks, standing row upon row. I didn't know I was supposed to remember the building number, my platoon number, and all that stuff! And now the rest of the guys in my platoon were probably all down at the PX or somewhere, having a good time, while I slaved away and was completely lost!

Depressed. Betrayed. Confused. I wanted out of here!

1. What was your first moment of *depression* when you arrived at boot camp?

2. Why do you suppose that we sometimes *assume* that everyone else has it better (whatever that means) than we do?

3. What lesson for life should I have learned early on from this opening-day experience (besides *never volunteering*)?

Note from the Commander.

Answer me quickly, O Lord, my spirit fails; Do not hide Your face from me, Or I will become like those who go down to the pit. Let me hear Your lovingkindness in the morning; For I trust in You; Teach me the way in which I should walk; For to You I lift up my soul. (Psalm 143:7-8 NASB)

11

The Haircut

Twenty-five cents?! I had to *pay* for this? Just who did they think they were?! At least he'd better cut it the way I liked it! It was funny watching the others get their hair cut. The reason it was cut so short was because they didn't tell the barber what they wanted. That wouldn't be a problem for me.

I was already used to a flat-top haircut anyway. I had one in high school, and I kept it in my brief stint in college. So this shouldn't really be a problem. He'd probably look at my haircut and pass me right on. I was feeling pretty smug. I had asked Mom to cut my hair just before I left home, so I would look good before I got here.

"Lifto, get in the chair!" I limped forward and sat down.

What was he doing?! His electric clippers were *shaving* my head! Hey, let me point out a few features I'd like to preserve! You just sat me down and took off! Now my head looked like a farmer without his tee shirt! A big lump of white with a face on it! It looked like a white swimming cap! This was awful! What kind of sadistic monster had they put in charge of the barber shop?!

Fifteen seconds. That's all it took for a haircut! "Next!"

I was still in the chair! He didn't even give me a mirror to make sure it was okay. And then I had to pay for it!

How humiliating! Now I looked like the rest of these poor slobs. What were they feeling depressed about? Just look at me!

It was kinda fun to look at Fred, though. He used to have a ducktail. We were still in our civilian clothes, and his collar was up. But he didn't look as cool as he used to, if you could imagine the Fonz with a white buzz clip.

1. What do you suppose the purposes are for everyone getting that same white buzz clip?

2. Isn't this kind of humiliation *disrespectful* to an American soldier?

3. Why do you suppose that some of the guys had "more to lose" with the haircut than the others?

Note from the Commander.

But I thought it necessary to send to you Epaphroditus, my brother and fellow worker and fellow soldier, who is also your messenger and minister to my need. (Philippians 2:25 NASB)

12

Getting the Uniform

All right! We were getting uniforms this afternoon! I'd be looking cool in that squared-off green uniform with the saucer cap and a few medals that I'd probably get in basic training, eh? Maybe I could get some sergeant stripes, too before I got done with basic.

What's this – an assembly line? Didn't I get to try on some of this stuff before I had to sign for it? Was this all the underwear we got? And why was our underwear green? I didn't like green underwear. And I didn't wear boxers! What did they mean that I couldn't wear my own underwear from home? And these green socks were scratchy! How was I supposed to get all this stuff in this one duffel bag?! Wouldn't it get all wrinkled up?

So …. Not enough changes of underwear. Sizes not right. No hangers. No starter medals or stripes. No washer or dryer in the barracks. And not enough room to put it anyway.

And where was our transportation? They couldn't expect me to lug all this stuff all the way back to the barracks, could they? What did they mean by *double-time*?!

Reception Station was staffed with sadistic rejects from another reality. I couldn't wait to start basic training just to get away from these guys. Wasn't Napoleon a corporal, too?! These snots weren't even sergeants. They acted this way because they were just losers on a power trip!

I was getting mad now. And I was only a couple of days in! But there was nothing I could do about it. Just wait till I was the sergeant! I'd show them a thing or two!

But wouldn't both Mom and Dad be proud when they saw me in this uniform?

1. Why do you suppose that the corporals and PFCs in Reception Station are on this power trip anyway?

2. What see-sawing in attitudes did you experience in your first days as a recruit?

3. What would you recommend to a potential recruit regarding his or her attitude during those initial days as a recruit?

Note from the Commander.

Devote yourselves to prayer, keeping alert in it with an attitude of thanksgiving. (Colossians 4:2 NASB)

13

Recruited Again!

"Who's got a high GT score[2]?"

Mine was pretty high, but I wasn't volunteering anything. The KP incident taught me to keep my head low. They probably were looking for some genius to operate a mop handle. But it looked like he had a lot of papers with lists of information on them anyway.

It turns out that, because of the Vietnam War going on, they were short of platoon sergeants to nursemaid soldiers through basic training. These weren't the drill sergeants, mind you. These were going to be the leaders, who would live in the barracks and be responsible for the platoon during basic training.

Didn't sound that worthwhile yet to me.

"You will get the platoon sergeant's room in the barracks. You'll wear this black armband with gold sergeant stripes on it and the LOC[3] logo on it. And your men, and all the staff in your basic training company will address you as 'sergeant.'"

---

[2] GT score was the old military forerunner of the IQ test. I think now there is something like an AFQT.
[3] Leadership Orientation Course.

Now they were talking! I'd get my dignity back! My own room instead of the open bay! And those cool sergeant stripes! Three days at the Reception Station, and I'd already be on top! So, I volunteered.

Then they told me. Another week after this one at Reception Station, waiting for LOC to begin for my group. Then a one-week crash course so I could lead others through basic training.

Another week ... here at the Reception Station? A crash course in basic training? I thought that basic training was already a crash course – and that was going to be eight weeks! Then, what was *this* course going to be like?! And this added another two weeks to my sentence at Ft. Leonard Wood! I'd *never* get home! I wonder if Mom missed me yet.

1. Why was I starting to view myself as such a *fool* or *sucker* in the Army?

2. Would you value this opportunity as a good one or a bad one for me at this point in my military career? Why?

3. Why do so many young people fail to recognize the value of the *sacrifice* that is required in order to accomplish something significant in their lives?

Note from the Commander.

Do nothing from selfishness or empty conceit, but with humility of mind regard one another as more important than yourselves. (Philippians 2:3)

14

So Broke

Mom gave me $10 to help me on my way. I had only a few bucks of my own to add to that. But where would $16 take me? I'd been away from home about a week now, with no money coming in.

The Army paid $76 a month, which would be plenty, but payday was still weeks away! No one told me in advance that I would have to do my own laundry or else pay for it. Mom used to do all of mine. I didn't know how to use an iron. Good grief, I didn't even own one!

And it looked like I needed shoe polish and a can of something called Brasso® and tooth powder and white towels and shaving soap and shaving brush[4] ... and lots of deodorant!

Ahhh! The trip down to Finance! Standing in line in parade rest was so easy, knowing that my name was going into the payroll record books!

---

[4] I didn't know what tooth powder was either. And I didn't know anybody that used a shaving brush. But we needed this stuff and a few towels under it to set up our display in the upper tray of our foot locker!

"Do you want advance pay?" I knew I could sure use $5 or so to get me through to the end of the month.

"Yes, sir."

"Okay. Ten dollars. Take this voucher to the line at the cage."

Ten dollars! That was enough to pay a week's rent in college! What would I do with ten dollars?!

1. Okay, how much did you earn per month in basic training? Were you used to having so much to spend, when the military took care of so many other things, such as room and board?

2. When did you begin to get the picture that maybe the military knew at least as much as you did about what you needed?

3. At your tender age as a fresh recruit, did you really understand what you needed in life?

Note from the Commander.

Give us each day our daily bread. (Luke 11:3 NASB)

15
The Old Recruit

Good grief, he must have been twenty-two or twenty-three years old. And he was just now joining the Army! Must have been a loser and couldn't get a job on the *outside*. Two years of college they say he had. He couldn't be that smart. But here we were in leadership orientation, preparing ourselves for leadership in basic training.

"Hang your dress greens in the bathroom, close to the shower. It'll get the wrinkles out!"

"Heat the polish before you use it, and it'll be softer and easier to put on the shoe!"

"Shower and shave at night, so you won't be so rushed and have to stand in line when you get up in the morning!"

"Don't wear your boots on the barracks linoleum. But keep your socks on, so the floor won't get so scuffed up, and buffing the floor in the morning will be easier!"

Man, where did he pick up this stuff? I stayed close to him! He seemed to have all his ducks in a row already! I felt like an idiot next to him, but I guess that was okay, because he was like a big brother to everyone in the barracks.

All I had were three younger brothers. And they looked up to me, I guess. But only because I was taller. But do old guys really know anything? I thought all they did was strut around and yell at you. Wow. What a strange experience.

1. Did you have a *big brother*? What were some of the benefits?

2. How about a grandpa or grandma? Did you ever listen to their advice? Should you have?

3. Was there ever someone in the military that you would deem a *mentor*?

Note from the Commander.
Accept my teaching. Learn from me. I am gentle and humble in spirit. And you will be able to get some rest. (Matthew 11:29 ERV)

16
Drill and Ceremonies

"Left h'ace! Forward h'arch! Your left right! Your left right let! Hut toop, threep, fourp! Your left right left!"

"To the rear – h'arch! Company – halt!"

"Left shoulder – h'arms! Present – h'arms!"

I got it! I could do that! I even had the voice!

I had no idea about the rifle stuff. I didn't know anything about keeping a barracks clean. I knew nothing about discipline – even my own. I couldn't polish a pair of boots. But I sure knew drill and ceremonies!

Why is it that there is someone in every platoon that can't keep the beat? They're always out of step. Can't they just follow the guy ahead of them? Why do they need to look down at their feet? Do they really believe that watching their feet will help? And it made the whole platoon look bad. People who can't march shouldn't be allowed to join the Army. They could never be real soldiers. Real soldiering was being able to make a strong, confident show of force ... in a parade.

I could stand at attention, feet at a 45-degree angle, hands at my sides, fingers curled correctly. I could hold my head back with a straight, cold, forward stare. I executed each move with a snap.

My dad would be proud. But I'd never talk with him about it. We didn't really talk about anything anyway.

Interesting. Maybe it was because it was so structured. Maybe it was because at least I was coordinated. Maybe it was because I could keep the beat. Maybe it was because I really wanted to be just like that strong exhibit of manhood that had paraded in front of me every Fourth of July as I was growing up. And now I was that very soldier.

I didn't know whether I could do much else yet in basic training. But I could sure march.

1. What did you think of the drill and ceremonies portion of basic training?

2. Was there anything in particular that you really excelled at in basic training? When did you know that you were going to be good at it?

3. What inspired you to become a soldier in the first place?

4. Did you ever think that God could make you into the person you could only dream about being?

Note from the Commander.

*And do not be conformed to this world, but be **transformed** by the renewing of your mind, so that you may prove what the will of God is, that which is good and acceptable and perfect.* (Romans 12:2 NASB)

17
The Daily Dozen

A dozen of them?! How could there be twelve different exercises that we needed to suffer through every morning? That was sheer torture! Pure agony!

And who could remember twelve different exercises anyway? The drill sergeants just called out for a demonstrator, and made him hold each position till he just about died. Then they ran him and the rest of us through enough repetitions that any of us would have volunteered to assassinate him.

And how was I supposed to keep cadence – out loud?! I could hardly breathe! Couldn't the drill sergeant just keep count for us all? But no-o-o. We had to count with him, really loud. He even wanted it louder and louder. What was wrong with that man?

And what was with the eight-count pushups? Why should I spend four of the counts getting down on the ground and getting back up, just to do two pushups? It wasn't very efficient.

And what was that body twist thing all about? I never could reach down and touch the top of my boots with my legs locked straight anyway. It isn't normal.

Now, I did enjoy the running around the track. Three miles it was in those days. But I could have done a better job if I could have worn my tennis shoes. I thought it was pretty stupid to run three miles in combat boots. They were too hot and heavy. And running shorts would be better than running in fatigues, too.

Exercise after exercise. Couldn't he see that we were getting tired? The drill sergeant wandered through the formation with a grin on his face, looking for wounded stragglers that he could pounce on. Why did he pick on the guys that were hardly hanging on? I'd show him! I never let him know I was in pain. He'd never see that my muscles were vibrating inside my sleeves. Not a tear.

Or was that what he wanted?

1. Did you ever figure out later that someone teaching you something *really* knew what he was doing, despite your frustrations while you were learning?

2. The rigors I went through in basic training likely saved my life while I was in Viet Nam. And I never remembered the name of a single drill sergeant. Which drill sergeant helped you the most?

Note from the Commander.

People tell silly stories that don't agree with God's truth. Don't follow what these stories teach. But teach yourself to be devoted to God. Training your body helps you in some ways. But devotion to God helps you in every way. It brings you blessings in this life and in the future life too. Here is a true statement that should be accepted without question. (1 Timothy 4:7-9 ERV)

18

Shiny Garbage Cans

My week in Leadership Orientation Course extended over Easter that year. In fact, Easter Sunday would be my last full day before graduation. And here it was Good Friday. And so, I figured there'd be a great breakfast, some announcements, and then a day of relaxation before we finished it all off over the weekend.

"Lifto, get over to the mess hall. You're up for KP!"

Hey, it was 5:00 in the morning! I was still in the shower! This wasn't fair! How could they give me KP on my graduation day? And it was a holiday! Didn't they know I was a Christian, and it was an important religious day for me to go to chapel? I think there was a chapel somewhere on post. I hadn't thought much about it before that moment, I guess.

"Don't just stand there, get out there and put a shine on those garbage cans!"

Put a shine on garbage cans? Was the mess sergeant some kind of psycho? I mean, mess hall garbage cans are supposed to smell bad and get caked up a bit, right? Back on the farm, we never scrubbed and shined up our pig slop bucket! I don't remember ever shining the manure fork!

Poor me. On my graduation day, I had KP. While everyone else was packing their bags and kicking back for the day, I was scrubbing garbage cans. And I smelled bad. Three weeks in the Army, and I had descended into the depths of despair. There is nothing worse in anyone's life than having KP on a holiday and scrubbing garbage cans.

I cried. I wanted to go home.

1. What was your lowest moment in your Army life? Was it as bad as KP on a holiday?

2. What do you suppose is the difference between breaking a young man's will and breaking his spirit? Which was broken in this case?

3. What advice would you have given a young recruit like me at that sad moment?

Note from the Commander.
Because of the tender mercy of our God,
With which the Sunrise from on high will visit us,
To SHINE UPON THOSE WHO SIT IN DARKNESS AND THE SHAD-
OW OF DEATH,
To guide our feet into the way of peace. (Luke 1:78-79 NASB)

19

Graduating from LOC

I was in a panic as I cleaned off the crud from KP, changed into my dress greens, and packed my bags. Graduation ceremonies from LOC would be in a few minutes, and I knew there would be an inspection in ranks before it began. No one helped me. They had plenty of their own problems to deal with. I can't figure out how in the world I got outside into formation on time, but I did.

First the parade. That was something I was great at. I had a proud march step, and could handle the rifle well. Every move I made had a snap to it. Feeling good!

I had learned how to strip down an M-14 and put it back together. I could perform any of the daily dozen exercise routines automatically. I knew all the basic marching and rifle commands. I could make a military bed with a tight square corner. I could already remember most of the basic military orders. I could properly wear the uniform and shine my own shoes. And I could operate the dish sprayer in the mess hall and scrub garbage cans. And I had learned all this in one week.

I wasn't really sure that I even needed to go through basic training! What more could there be? It would be a cake walk.

Three weeks in the Army, and I was already a sergeant ... well, sort of. The black arm band with the gold sergeant stripes and the gold LOC symbol superseding it all – it looked really good, high up there on my left arm. I was probably as good as a *real* sergeant already anyway.

And then my turn came. I stepped in line across the podium, I saluted the captain, and he passed me my graduation certificate. They probably would want me to give a speech. Well, maybe not.

Wouldn't Mom be proud!

1. Did you ever have an ego problem early on in your military career?

2. What skills did you think you had mastered, but later discovered that you really barely had a clue about?

3. Why do you suppose we like to make our mothers proud of us?

Note from the Commander.
*What people say about themselves means nothing. What counts is whether the Lord says they have **done well**.* (2 Corinthians 10:18)

20

Impressing the Company Staff

Running the track

Okay, I'd been assigned to C Company. Funny how the staff there greeted us better than at the Reception Station. There were only four of us from Leadership Orientation Course assigned to the company, but we lined up in a small formation anyway, as quickly as we could pile off from the bus that brought us there.

The captain actually shook hands with us! So did the senior sergeants of the company. It was like they treated us as fellow professionals! They even addressed me as "Sergeant Lifto!"

They looked us over a bit, and pointed to a makeshift running track. It seemed as though the question of the day wasn't about how smart we were, but what condition we were in. There were questions about how many pushups we could do, and how quickly we could run a mile. Other than the daily dozen, we never searched for the limits on either of these. However, I did pride myself in knowing the steps and procedures of each exercise if they wanted me to quote them.

But over to the makeshift track we went. Somehow, I forgot to pack my gym clothes or running shoes. Maybe we'd have a chance to get over to the PX and get some before we had to do anything overly strenuous.

What did they mean, "Take off your blouse!" Oh, in the Army the outer shirt is called a blouse. Kind of a sissy name as far as I was concerned. But surely we didn't have to run in our combat boots and in fatigues!

Wrong again! Now back on the farm, I could run the hills through the woods like the deer who lived there. But not in combat boots! And it had been several months since I had been in the woods running. But this seemed like some kind of proving ground for the company staff about my manhood.

So, I let it all hang out. I sprinted right from the starting line, building up nearly a half lap on the next guy behind me. Oh, a second lap? Okay, but maybe not quite as fast as the first one. I started breathing a little heavier, but maintained my lead. What? A third lap? It seemed that a mile was a bit farther than I had thought! I paced myself on this one. The others were gaining quickly, but my lead was still enough to finish in front of all of them.

One more lap? Were they nuts? My legs could hardly move anymore! The boots weighed at least fifteen pounds each now. I was gasping for a breath every two steps as I heard the pounding of boots directly behind me. But this was the one thing that I could do well. Others were stronger than me. Others may have been smarter. But I *thought* that I could run. And so, I quit thinking about the pain. I started thinking about the embarrassment of starting out way ahead, and then possibly finishing last. I would burn it all on this last lap. And I made it.

Vomiting doesn't count, does it?

1. What have you discovered about the varying expectations of you by different people? Have you been able to meet all their expectations?

2. Tell us a story about your "proving ground," where you had to prove that you had what it takes.

3. Give us your opinion of maybe two or three things you believe it takes to demonstrate that you are a *real* man.

Note from the Commander.

We have all these great people around us as examples. Their lives tell us what faith means. So we, too, should run the race that is before us and never quit. We should remove from our lives anything that would slow us down and the sin that so often makes us fall. (Hebrews 12:1 ERV)

21
Welcoming the Recruits

Here came the buses! Look at those scared recruits! I'd straighten them out pretty quick.

"Get off that bus! Come on, I don't have all day! Let's go, you clowns! Pick up that bag! Get into formation! Good grief, don't you know anything?!"

Oh, the adrenalin rush! I felt like a junkie with a power injection! Those sergeant stripes on my left arm transformed me into a god! Look how they jumped at my command! Watch them squirm when I yelled at them. This was better than picking on my little sister!

Yeah, she whined pretty much, and sometimes even cried when I picked on her. But then I'd get punished for it. In fact, when she wanted her way, she learned that all she had to do was whine really loud, and Dad would come running to coddle her and to brutalize me.

But now, there was no retribution. Now I could get away with it. Now I could push people around, and my skinny size and my formerly shy, diminutive personality had completely vanished. I had the stripes. That meant my power was absolute. I was reveling in it! And I had no sympathy whatsoever for the poor schnooks that would have to suffer under my feet.

No sympathy. It's a cold world out there, and they'd better learn to take it. When they were in combat, no one would coddle them. And they would soon learn that whining was not an option!

Was I a bully? No; this was the way bosses were supposed to talk! It was the way my Dad talked, and he was a line boss at the shoe factory. It was all about showing people who was tough … or so I thought.

1. Do you think that something may have been missing from my leadership training before I was awarded the temporary sergeant stripes? What, specifically?

2. Do you ever wonder why some authority figures in the military seem to become little Napoleons when they've been given authority?

3. How do you suppose a soldier needs to modify his behavior when he deals with his wife? His children?

Note from the Commander.
When you talk, you should always be kind and wise. Then you will be able to answer everyone in the way you should. (Colossians 4:5 ERV)

22
Zero Week

Zero week! What did they mean by *zero week?*! Basic training was supposed to be eight weeks long! I had already spent two weeks at the Reception Station instead of one. And I spent yet another week at Leadership Orientation Course. And now I discovered that eight weeks of basic training started with an additional week called "zero week" before the other eight were counted!

I was starting not to like my Army contract one bit!

When would all this spy stuff start? I'd bet James Bond never got treated like this. I thought that when I started working for the government, everything would finally start going smoothly. The government hired experts. The government was efficient. The government knew it shouldn't waste valuable resources. Maybe someone in the front office didn't get the memo about me. Let's get on with it!

Three weeks already, and I hadn't even begun basic training yet. Here I was, 2000 miles away from home (well, maybe 400 miles). I didn't have any friends. I kept getting shipped around post. I didn't even know my way around the company area. What did they expect from me?

1. Have you ever been homesick? What did you miss back home?

2. When you were homesick, did you have a feeling that you were missing events that were occurring while you were away, and that the world back home was changing without you?

3. Do you think that homesickness is somehow a part of the right of passage from being a boy, and growing into a man? How so?

Note from the Commander.

Then Cain said to the Lord, "This punishment is more than I can bear! You are forcing me to leave the land, and I will not be able to be near you or have a home! Now I must wander from place to place, and anyone I meet could kill me." Then the Lord said to cain, "no, if anyone kills you, i will punish that person much, much more." then the Lord put a mark on Cain to show that no one should kill him. (Genesis 4:13-15 ERV)

23
My Foul Mouth!

"G-d... you! Get out of bed!"

That got him moving! Nobody in my platoon would ever get the notion that this was just a bunch of fun and games. When I said something, I expected action!

"What the h--- do you think you're doing?! I showed you how I want you to disassemble your weapon. Put a towel under it, or you'll lose the pieces all over the floor!"

That felt kinda funny. The words just slipped out. In fact, they started coming out easier and easier as time went on.

Dad swore all the time. Mom thought it was terrible, even sacrilegious. Maybe it was. But without Mom around, it seemed easy. And nobody seemed to mind. At least no one said anything about it. And it seemed like the vocabulary that tough GIs must use. And I certainly wanted to sound like a tough GI! And it would probably help me gain the respect I needed as a leader over my platoon.

And so, I inserted profanity into just about everything I said. If anything, no one would mistake that I knew how to use the words and I was unafraid to stick them into any conversation I wanted to.

Of course, I wouldn't go to the Bible study that somebody put together in the Day Room. Or attend chapel, which was too boring compared to the Baptist church back home anyway. Besides, if I went to either, then the guys might get the wrong impression. Like maybe I was some kind of pansy or something.

I felt a little guilty about it, though.

1. Did you ever have a boss with a foul mouth? Did it increase your fear of him? Did it increase your respect for him?

2. Why do you suppose a lot of guys fall into the trap of relating a foul mouth with masculinity?

3. What advice or training would you have advised an immature temporary recruit sergeant like me?

Note from the Commander.

The mouth of the righteous utters wisdom, And his tongue speaks justice. Psalm 37:30 On account of the sin of their mouth and the words of their lips, Let them even be caught in their pride, And on account of curses and lies which they utter. Psalm 59:12 NASB *That you should turn your spirit against God And allow such words to go out of your mouth?* (Job 15:13 NASB)

Let the words of my mouth and the meditation of my heart Be acceptable in Your sight, O Lord, my rock and my Redeemer. (Psalm 19:14 NASB)

24

A Coke From the Drill Sergeant

The end of drill that Saturday finally came. Zero Week was over. SFC Woszanski wanted to see me.

He was one of the drill instructors, and I was one of two platoon sergeants assigned directly under him. I can't remember how to spell his name, maybe because there were so many letters in it. He smoked a lot. Maybe I'd take that habit up pretty soon also. But I didn't like going down to the PX, and taking care of the cigarettes and lighter and all that seemed like more trouble than it was worth at the time.

Anyway, SFC Woszanski wanted to see me alone – over by the Coke machine just outside the Day Room. What did I do? And if I couldn't think of the problem ahead of time, how would I think up a good excuse for it?

"Want a Coke?" It was a trap! The Coke machine was off limits while we were in training!

"Well, I don't know about that," I choked out.

"That's okay. Training's over for the week."

"Oh, yeah. Sure, that would be okay." What was going on? Was he setting me up for a dressing down? No one gives anything away without some kind of motive, right?

"Where you from, Lifto?"

"Minnesota."

"Do you come from a big family?"

"Yes. Two sisters and three brothers."

"Any hobbies?"

"No time. I was going to college." I sure wasn't going to tell him that I played the violin!

The repartee continued for about five minutes before he said he had to take off for the day. I survived! What was he digging for? Why was he prying in my personal business anyway?

Funny thing though. He seemed to care.

1. Were you ever on your guard when a superior called you out for a little discussion?

2. What do you suppose was SFC Woszanski's motive for talking with me?

3. Is there possible something in some guys' backgrounds that cause them to always suspect some ulterior motive?

Note from the Commander.
I am the Good Shepherd. I know my own sheep and my own sheep know me. In the same way, the Father knows me and I know the Father. (John 10:14-15 MSG)

25
Sunday Chapel

It was Easter Sunday. We graduated from the leadership course. I was assigned to C Company and had run the mile for them. And it was still Sunday morning. The fresh recruits would be arriving early that afternoon. What else did they have in store for us acting sergeants that morning?

"Get your greens on. You're volunteering for chapel!"

Huh? I was "volunteering" to go to chapel? Mom was hoping I'd go, of course. But it probably wouldn't be the same as like back home, where I knew people and we could goof around before and after the service. But I was good at this, whatever that meant. So, I could show the others what a good church participant I could be. My attendance back home at the Baptist Church, reluctant though it may have been, would come in handy today.

Hey, wait a minute! What kind of music was this?! They were all a bunch of soldier anthems! What happened to "When the Rolls Are Served Up Yonder, I'll Be There" and fun songs like that? Why were there drill sergeants sauntering up and down the aisles, glowering at us, and straightening up the few soldiers who were slouching a bit? This was like going to church with my dad! He would interrupt my brother and me during worship to fix our ties, to stop us from whispering, or to wipe the grins off our faces. I didn't think I'd "volunteer" for chapel in the future.

Well, that was the only chapel service I was ever required to attend. And indeed, during the next nearly four years, I'd attend chapel only a few more times, usually on holidays because someone else asked me along.

Nothing much there for me. Of course, I wouldn't tell Mom about my absence from the throne of God!

1. Did you ever attend a chapel worship service? What did you like about it? What didn't you like?

2. Did you ever feel guilty about not attending? Was there someone you didn't want to know about your lack of religion?

3. What would it take for you to be willing to give it another shot? Is there another church you could attend without it seeming so "military"?

Note from the Commander.

And let us consider how to stimulate one another to love and good deeds, not forsaking our own assembling together, as is the habit of some, but encouraging one another; and all the more as you see the day drawing near. (Hebrews 10:24-25 NASB)

26
Mail Call!

"Johnson, Fred; Wilson, John; Marik, Roger; Bartholomew, Samuel!" On and on the supply sergeant shouted, as we all crowded around his front door. He had the day's mail, and was passing it out. Well, he was sort of *passing* it out. He'd call a name, then Frisbee-toss the letter in the general direction of the voice that replied, "Here, Sergeant!"

What a frustrating event. There was no alphabetical order. It took all of five minutes, but five minutes lasted an eternity, when there was no guarantee of any word from home. On days when there was no letter, which was most of them, we would put on this nonchalant face. You know, the one that says: "It doesn't matter; I didn't need a letter anyway."

Some guys got letters from their girlfriends. I didn't like them very much. Those guys were probably cocky and thought highly of themselves. Then there were the guys that got a coffee can fun of cookies and candy from home. They tended to share it, which was nice. I'd have to remember to do that if I ever got one.

"Lifto, Clayton!" Hey, that was me! A letter! From Mom, of course. To this day, I can't think of anyone else who would possibly have written me a letter. My friends were guys, and guys don't write letters.

It was so great. Handwritten. The words and the lines small and crowded together, every space filled with words, even notes in the margins. News about the ducks and chickens. News about the cows and the barn. News about the garden. News about my brothers and sisters. News about my friends. News about church. There were jokes clipped out and stuffed in the envelope.

And there were religious tracts. That was Mom. She never forgot me. She never forgot any of her six children. She thought about me and prayed for me every day. What was wrong with her? Well, it was cool to get the letters.

1. How has mail call changed from the way mine worked back in the mid-sixties?

2. Why do you suppose it was so important for this eighteen-year-old GI to get a letter from home?

3. What do you suppose Mom had in mind when she kept sending me those tracts?

Note from the Commander.
(A song by Cindy Morgan "Will You Be There?")
I do not want to walk through Heaven's gates
and not see your face
And I do not want to dance beside the streams

Without you with me
Or See the angels fill the sky
The Heaven's sing and all creation cries
Hosanna, Savior, God our Father
Creator, Oh Savior and King
You've got to be there with me
Oh, Please You've got to be there with me
Will you be there with me?

27
Pay Call!

How was this going to work? How would I cash my huge paycheck when we weren't allowed to leave the company area? Would the PX even have enough cash to handle it?

Let's see, I got $76 a month, less just a few days since I started on April 5th. There was that $10 partial pay that they gave me at the Reception Center. But still that left quite a pile!

What would I do with it all? They paid for all my food. I didn't have any car to pay for, or any loans. Maybe some laundry soap and money for the weekly cleaners for my uniforms, but that was about it.

"Fall out and assemble in a line at the Day Room in alphabetical order!" Oh, so this was how it went! They paid in cash and gave us a receipt.

There were stations at makeshift desks set in a row. First I signed a receipt for the money I received. Then I saluted an officer and he counted out my $58 that remained after deductions. At the next table, labeled Soldier's Home, a sergeant barked,

"Two dollars!" I dished out two dollars and stepped sideways over to the next table with the sign Red Cross. "Two dollars!" I handed over two dollars as I shuffled out the door. Who knows how many more tables another twenty years would bring!

I experienced three such pay calls during basic training, and only a few more like that at my next assignment. A huge pile of money at the beginning of the month: desperate poverty leading up to the next pay line.

I don't know where it went. I never seemed to know where it went.

1. What positive changes did you experience in the pay system since my time – and the amount of pay itself?

2. What do you think of the old military method of obtaining contributions for good causes?

3. Did you ever feel as though you were loaded – flush with cash?

Note from the Commander.
Woe to him who builds his house without righteousness and his upper rooms without justice, who uses his neighbor's services without pay and does not give him his wages. (Jeremiah 22:13 NASB)

28
No Weekend Passes!

We kept hearing about Waynesville. It must have been some kind of thriving metropolis that catered to all the needs of a soldier! We heard the stories. There were hundreds and hundreds, maybe thousands, of young, beautiful single women, looking for lonely GIs in basic training, starving for dates and yearning for love!

Restaurants there catered to GIs in basic training--the pie was free, and they were open all night – or so I had heard. Bars were fun; you could drink all night without getting drunk, and they gave free rides back to the barracks – or so I had heard.

I just had to get there! I wasn't sure why. I hadn't been successful in my dating life. In fact, I'd never actually asked a girl for a date yet. There were the two Sadie Hawkins Day dates in high school. One took me bowling, which was a total embarrassment. I had never bowled prior to that. My first game that night I only scored a 32. It got to be that a crowd gathered around my each shot, coaxing the ball down the three-mile-long lane, praying it wouldn't wobble into the gutter. Utter shame. The other Sadie Hawkins date was a church party. Oh, well.

Maybe it was that Waynesville represented an escape from this eternal military prison. Maybe I'd just walk around downtown a bit. Maybe I'd just sleep without someone barking at me. I don't know. I just wanted to get away.

So, here we were in afternoon formation. And then all the announcements. After Week 4, there would be the possibility of weekend passes! They would draw two names each week. Two names! Out of about 160 guys! No hope. And indeed … I never got a weekend pass during my entire three months at Fr. Leonard Wood, Missouri.

It was bittersweet. I wouldn't get away from the confinement of the restriction to the company area. But I would remain safe in a prison I had grown comfortable in.

1. Where was your Waynesville in basic training? Was the town all that it was cracked up to be?

2. Is a basic trainee actually better off without taking a weekend pass during training?

3. How do we sometimes build a zone of safety around ourselves, where we're comfortable, and don't feel a need to go outside or leave it?

Note from the Commander.
You shall fear only the LORD your God; and you shall worship Him and swear by His name. (Deuteronomy 6:13 NASB)

29
The Day Room

Why do they call it a "Day Room"? No one is allowed in there during the day anyway, except for Sundays. It was just a dinky wooden building built on a slab. A TV that only got one channel, a few plastic-covered couches, and a bumper pool table – that was about it. Oh, yes, there was a card table, too – with three chairs. The fourth one was always broken or missing.

It was a place to hang out on Sunday afternoons. All the other days and nights were so busy that no one ever visited there. But on Sunday afternoons, the Day Room was the place to be. We'd sprawl out on the concrete floor where we could find room, listen to the raucous stories, laugh at the appropriate moments, and shrug with indifference whenever their stories seemed beyond your own personal experience.

Why was everyone else's life more interesting than mine? I was eighteen years old and didn't even have a driver's license. I had never been drunk. In fact the most alcohol I ever consumed was from Dad's empty beer cans, just tasting the last drop that was left over if I was patient enough and clever enough for it to reach my lips. I'd never had a girlfriend. Oh, there was one who might have worked out, had I the courage to ever ask her. But I didn't. These guys seemed to have already procured their own private harems!

It kind of made me wonder about my own upbringing. I grew up on a farm that was mostly woods and hills. I could wander through forests of birch trees on one day and maples the next. I could slide down the hills on drifts of autumn leaves that filled the furrowed valleys between the knolls. I could sit with Rex, my dog, and gaze for miles across valleys and hills, flocked with the colors of each of the Minnesota seasons.

But that life didn't play well in the Day Room. I didn't know much about drinking, women, or pool. And that's what life was all about, right?

1. Was I missing something here? What was it?

2. How did your upbringing help prepare you for life in basic training? What did you lack?

3. What would you advise this young man about whose voice to listen to, and peer pressure?

Note from the Commander.

Summing it all up, friends, I'd say you'll do best by filling your minds and meditating on things true, noble, reputable, authentic, compelling, gracious—the best, not the worst; the beautiful, not the ugly; things to praise, not things to curse. Put into practice what you learned from me, what you heard and saw and realized. Do that, and God, who makes everything work together, will work you into his most excellent harmonies. (Philippians 4:8-9 The Message)

30
Road Marches and Bivouac

At breakfast formation the announcements were usually brief. We reported that everyone was accounted for. We'd maybe do some calisthenics, then the first sergeant told us about the day's training schedule.

When he announced the rifle range, or anything else with the word "range" in it, everyone groaned, because we knew that it meant several miles each way on a road march over gravel roads.

I myself loved road marches. Maybe it was because I had spent so much time growing up out in the country, exploring back trails and hiking in the woods. And another thing – no one bugged me while we were on the march. Once in a while a drill sergeant would decide we should all sing a road march song. And that was annoying. I hated singing those stupid ditties! They were these short, moronic poems to keep our minds off our tiring legs. There was something about esprit de corps, too, whatever that was. Couldn't a guy just walk down the road in peace?!

And toward the end of basic training, we road marched so far that we had to camp overnight! I guess it was to make sure we could put together those shelter halves and see if we could sleep with another guy without getting upset with each other. Too bad that it dumped rain that night. And too bad that we didn't see any need to use our entrenching tool, otherwise known as a folding shovel, to dig a couple of water trenches around our shelter to prevent the river washing down the side of the hill from drenching us and all our equipment. And, of course, we wouldn't say anything about it, or we'd catch the wrath of the drill sergeant, who would explain to us how stupid we were and allow us to practice making proper water trenches for the next several hours.

And breakfast would be just swell that morning, too. We lined up with our little mess kits that folded up with our canteens. The pouring rain helped thin out the scrambled eggs and float the sausages. And with nowhere to sit in the eating area, where the mud was so heavy that you had to curl your toes to keep your boots from getting sucked off, you had to eat standing up.

I was so glad I joined the Army.

1. Can you remember any of the marching songs or "ditties" from when you were in basic training?

2. Describe a time in basic training when rain was a problem. How did you cope with it?

3. How has the military improved on eating meals out in the field from the mid-sixties when I was there?

Note from the Commander.

But you, be sober in all things, endure hardship, do the work of an evangelist, fulfill your ministry. (2 Timothy 4:5 NASB)

31
NBC Training

Oh, this would be fun. Another boring lecture about what happens if we had a nuclear, biological, or chemical attack. There hadn't been any of those since WWI, as far as I knew. And we probably would survive anyway, so why bother?

Sure, they had these little display houses where they would open a canister of tear gas. But our masks were able to withstand that anyway, so big deal. Of course, I did hear that they made you take off your mask while inside, but I'd just close my eyes and hold my breath for that part.

Why were so many guys piling out of the building coughing and gagging? Some of them even vomited. Why didn't they just hold their breath until the "all clear" signal? Man, they were stupid!

As it was our turn to file into the building, I started getting a little nervous. Had I adjusted the straps to my mask correctly? Would my lumpy face with the zits allow the mask to seal okay, especially when I was sweating profusely? And why weren't we allowed to put on the masks before we went in?

"Mask!" the order exploded. Hey, I wasn't ready! I was already a second behind, and we were only given seven seconds to get it on. I could already hear the canister hissing. If I didn't get it on quick, I'd probably be gagging pretty soon. And the panic made it even more difficult to hold my breath for very long! A slap on the cheek nozzles and the chin, and I drew my first breath. It was okay. Oh, the feeling of relief!

"Clear!" We could take them off and put them back into their cases.

What was that hissing sound? Where was the order to "mask"?! This must be the *experiential* part, when I closed my eyes and held my breath! I could do that. I wasn't that stupid. Come on, that's long enough! Why were they letting out only the ones that were gagging! They were going to hold me in here until I got a good dose of tear gas! How could I escape the gas?! Could I *pretend* to gag? Never mind – vomit worked just fine.

1. What was your NBC training experience like?

2. Did you ever think you could "beat the system" in basic training? How did it work for you?

3. Which lectures did you consider the most boring and inapplicable? Why?

Note from the Commander.
Pride goeth before destruction, and an haughty spirit before a fall.
(Proverbs 16:18 KJV)

32
The Grenade Toss

They had a special range set up just for us to toss grenades! What was that all about? I mean, I grew up down by the creek, where my brother Jimmy and I picked up all kinds of rocks and tossed them at birds and squirrels and any other target that seemed appealing at the time. This wouldn't be so tough.

First they had to give us the lecture about how dangerous it was, and all that. Then they gave us a demonstration of different ways to stand and throw it. Then, of course, we tried it with dummy grenades that wouldn't even go off. What a waste of time!

Then it was finally my turn for the grenade toss with a real grenade. We had to stand behind a five-foot-high cement wall, toss the grenade at a target about fifteen yards out, then duck down again. Fine, no problem. The sergeant seemed a little nervous when he handed me the grenade, though. I gripped the grenade around the lever and pulled the pin.

"Throw it! Throw it!" he shouted at me. Good grief, what

was the hurry? The five-second timer didn't start until I released the lever, which I still gripped closed in my hand.

So I lobbed it over the wall. Okay, maybe I should have remembered that the target was about fifteen yards out. And maybe the lob was a bit too casual. But it cleared the wall … barely.

He grabbed my collar and yanked me to the ground just before it exploded!

"Boom!" And then the dirt and flak flying over the wall! Boy, was that something! And man, was the sergeant mad!

He wouldn't let me try another one.

1. Did you ever have a major goof-up that scared the boss a bit?

2. What could the instructors have done to help me grasp the seriousness of the boring safety training?

3. What is it about adrenalin rushes that make a guy want to try it again?

Note from the Commander.

So foolish was I, and ignorant: I was as a beast before thee. (Psalm 73:22 KJV)

O God, thou knowest my foolishness; and my sins are not hid from thee. (Psalm 69:5 KJV)

My wounds stink and are corrupt because of my foolishness. (Psalm 38:5 KJV)

33

The Rifle Range

I really enjoyed shooting. When I was barely twelve years old, my younger brother and I already had BB guns. We shot pigeons in the barn for the cats to feast on. We shot old Mason jars up in the woods. We even shot each other when we got mad enough.

And only a few years after that, we got a .22 rifle. Now we could really make those Mason jars explode! And what a noise we could make when we shot at squirrels as the bang ricocheted off the valley walls. We didn't mind it when Mom got perturbed with us around the house and would suggest to us, "Why don't you go shoot your rifles!"

And I could shoot well, too. I learned to squeeze the trigger as the bead of the leading sight settled into the crotch of the rear one. I could adjust for distance and even for the anomalies of the rifle itself. Jimmy's stupid rifle, for example, always shot down and to the left of anything he aimed at.

So, the rifle range would be kinda fun, I thought. And surely I would do well when it came to weapons qualification day. Too bad I over-oiled my M14 because of the expected rain that day. Too bad that my glasses fogged over with the chill of the morning, and beaded up with every drop of water that hit my face. Too bad that every round I fired threw yet another glob of oil onto my already slimy lenses. Too bad that I could rarely find the silhouette that popped up on time to even aim at it, let alone hit it.

It would be a year later before I had the opportunity to requalify. In the meantime I would be wearing the M14 Marksman badge, better dubbed, by those who knew, "the bolo badge" because it was the lowest qualification there was, with Sharpshooter and Expert being the higher levels of marksmanship.

Well, Mom probably wouldn't know the difference.

1. My Mom, later in life, around the age of seventy-eight, even joined the NRA. What were your mother's feelings about sending her children alone into the woods to shoot rifles?

2. What kind of excuses did you have for not shooting at the expert level at the rifle range ... like any *real* man would have?

3. What other badges are we sometimes forced to wear around on our uniforms that parallel in some way like my *bolo badge*?

Note from the Commander.

You know that in a race all the runners run, but only one runner gets the prize. So run like that. Run to win! All who compete in the games use strict training. They do this so that they can win a prize—one that doesn't last. But our prize is one that will last forever. So I run like someone who has a goal. I fight like a boxer who is hitting something, not just the air. It is my own body I fight to make it do what I want. I do this so that I won't miss getting the prize myself after telling others about it. (1 Corinthians 9:24-27 ERV)

34

The Concertina Range

Maybe it was actually called the "live fire range." I don't recall for sure. All I remember was that it was loaded with concertina wire, both in the rolls and the kind where they stake it out, zig-zagged just high enough to get your butt under it in a low crawl.

There were M60 machine guns set up behind us that were fired at three feet off the ground over our shoulders. Every fifth round was a red tracer, evidently designed to remind us not to stand up to scratch ourselves.

I forgot what the distance was that we were supposed to crawl through and under and around the obstacles. Maybe it was less than a hundred yards. But it seemed like a lot more than that. Probably it was only forty yards.

And the drill sergeants yelled at us the whole way. Things like, "Get down!" "Get moving!" "Get your butt down!" "Get your barrel out of the dirt!" "Quit your whimpering!" Things like that.

I wasn't really sure I understood what this exercise was all about. When would I ever have to crawl under concertina wire under fire? They told me I was going to be a linguist and a spy and I'd wear a tie every day! This looked more like combat stuff that would be for the infantry-type soldier than for a guy like me.

Maybe I should have brought this to the drill sergeant's attention.

And wasn't this all a little risky? I mean, real bullets and all that! What if something bad happened out there? They could get sued for reckless endangerment, right?

1. Was there any particular part of basic training that you deemed entirely inappropriate? Why?

2. How do you suppose my objections might have been received had I dared to raise them? Were there ever any objections that you raised that seemed to fall on deaf ears?

3. Of what value is any training--this training, for example--when it's unlikely you'll use it directly later in life? (By the way, read *Volume 4 – Vietnam* for better insights.)

Note from the Commander.
Be ready in season and out of season; reprove, rebuke, exhort, with great patience and instruction. (2 Timothy 4:2 NASB)

35
The PT Test

Three hundred points--that's all we needed to pass, out of five hundred points possible. There was the grenade throw, the low crawl, the hand-over-hand ladder, the run-dodge-and-jump, and the one-mile run – each event worth one hundred points. I could pass that! (Interesting, at my current age, I'd keel over in exhaustion just watching the events take place!) It was quite an exciting day. The company commander was there. We rarely saw him at all – maybe two or three times during the entire basic training cycle. And many NCOs from I don't where were there to score each event. Yup, this was a big day. Our company alone had 160 soldiers to be tested. And there were about four other companies in our battalion to be tested that day.

I had a little struggle with the grenade throw. They weren't live grenades, but I had a tendency to lob them like a hook shot in basketball. And they tended to drop quite a bit short.

I had a little trouble with the low crawl, too. It was twenty yards down, and the same twenty yards back. The scorer had trouble recognizing that my butt indeed was down. Maybe it just looked up in the air because it protruded a little.

Well, the hand-over-hand ladder didn't go all that well either. I wasn't expecting to be quite so sweaty. But it was testing day, and it was a hot day in late June. My hands were slippery.

The run-dodge-and-jump didn't go too badly, though. We had to jump across a hole, run to a wall, circle around it, run back, and jump back across the hole – twice. I would have even done a lot better if it hadn't been for that lump of dirt at the edge of the hole that tripped me up.

But the one-mile run was my event. It's really too bad that it was the last of the five events, and I was already pretty tired. Really, who wants to run fully dressed in their combat boots for an entire mile after they're already worn out from four other events?

Well, I passed.

1. How does today's Physical Training test differ from the one I had to take back in the sixties? Did you have one particular portion that seemed to have your name on it?

2. How well do you perform under the stress of a test? What do you tend to do to compensate?

3. What would you suggest to a young soldier that will be tested in many ways – even before he or she decides to enter the military?

Note from the Commander.

Do not be afraid; for God has come in order to test you, and in order that the fear of Him may remain with you, so that you may not sin. (Exodus 20:20 NASB)

Every word of God is tested; He is a shield to those who take refuge in Him. (Proverbs 30:5 NASB)

36
Graduation Day

Oh, the glory of it all! Hundreds--no, thousands of young soldiers passing in parade. And in the grandstand was somebody important ... I guess. It must have been a general, and maybe a Congressman, and then the bunch of hangers-on, who love to be seen with other people that are important.

And there I was, the young and dashing acting sergeant, with his rainbow ribbon[5] and bolo badge displayed proudly on his chest for the appreciative crowd to view. I loved drill and ceremonies, and this was Graduation Day.

Four members of our company were promoted to pay grade E2. That was still less than a PFC, but it meant a jump in pay to $84 a month, or more than 10% after only three months on duty. But the guys who got the promotion were not the acting sergeants like me. They were the ones who maxed the PT test!

So, brains and leadership weren't the criteria! It was physical

---

[5] Note that, since we were at war in Vietnam, a ribbon was awarded to all who served during that era, that resembled the colors of the rainbow. It was considered about the lowest award a service member could receive at the time – a ribbon for having completed basic training – wow.

prowess! Just like high school again! Academic proficiency meant nothing about popularity. It was always the jocks who got the attention and the prize. Nothing had changed! Only a year or two later, the military would offer up to E3 for a soldier with up to a year of college. I had completed a semester (sort of), so that should have counted for something!

But that mattered little now. I looked good out there on the parade ground. For sure, the general or the Congressman would notice me and how good I looked and how well I marched. So, I'd give them a good show with my shoulders set proudly and my snappy marching.

I wished Mom were there to see me.

1. What is the purpose of a Graduation Parade and Review? Was it for the soldier, or was it for the dignitaries?

2. Were any of your relatives able to make it to your basic training graduation? Why did you want them there?

3. Why do you suppose that Class A, formal military uniforms of each branch of service look so good?

Note from the Commander.

There are three things which are stately in their march,
Even four which are stately when they walk:
The lion which is mighty among beasts
And does not retreat before any,
The strutting rooster, the male goat also,
And a king when his army is with him. (Proverbs 30:29-31 NASB)

37
Riding Home on the Bus

They gave me two weeks' leave and three days' travel time to get to my next station, the Defense Language Institute, Monterey, California. That would give me plenty of time to get home, see my friends, and be on my way again.

Waynesville, Missouri didn't look like that big of a town. I'm glad I bought my ticket right there on post. I didn't bother to get off the bus while we stopped in town to load more passengers. I don't even remember what route we took to get to St. Paul. From there I took the next Greyhound down Highway 61 to Red Wing, Minnesota – home again.

The whole trip was surreal. I had been in a cage for so long, herded from one imprisonment to the next, that the whole idea of being set free, if only for a few weeks, just seemed incomprehensible to me.

Would my family have all changed? Would they recognize me? Would anyone be happy to see me? Did anyone miss me at all?

What would I do for those two weeks? There would be the Fourth of July parade. I'd make sure I wore my uniform for that. Then there was church on Sunday. I'd wear my uniform for that, too, of course.

I'd have to buy some more civilian clothes, that was for sure. I had only the shirt and pants that I'd worn down to Missouri, and they didn't fit anymore. I'd still stick out in a crowd, though. My hair was so short that I'd probably get a sunburn on the top of my head if I stayed outside too long in the sun.

Everyone would know that I was probably in the service. And the military wasn't that popular in those days.

1. What was going through your mind on the way home from basic training?

2. Did you want to strut your military self, or did you want to keep low during your home leave after basic? Why?

3. Who was there to meet you when you got home? The fact that people gave you a homecoming – what did that mean to you?

Note from the Commander.

So he got up and came to [i]*his father. But while he was still a long way off, his father saw him and felt compassion for him, and ran and* [j]*embraced him and kissed him. (Luke 15:20 NASB)*

Post Script

No, it's not over! Your story continued, didn't it? And so did mine. Let's grab *Volume 2* and keep going!

Just a note for you to consider, though.

Did you ever believe that all these experiences that each of has gone through have a meaning and purpose? I mean, these things really mature a man, don't they? It's interesting to me how as kids, we have these great dreams about life. And when reality hits us, we climb out of the dream and into the real world.

The truth is that none of us is perfect. We each have our issues and problems. Life isn't easy. But we struggle on.

Would you let this old retired sarge pass on some wisdom that was given to me many years ago by someone wiser than I was at the time? Would you just give it a quick read?

You know, none of us knows for sure what will happen to us here on earth until it occurs. We may die a hero in battle. We may die of old age, forgotten by all, wasting away in a nursing home somewhere.

You might have noticed at the bottom of each short story or vignette, that there was a brief "Note from the Commander." Those notes were provided as a word of encouragement. They aren't my words. They are God's words, straight from the Bible itself. Nowadays it's hard to know who to believe anymore. But at least these words we can trust.

As for me, I've even made a lot of money, then blew it all away. But no one can ever take away from me the love, joy, and peace that live inside of me. Take away my money, throw me in jail, beat me and harass me, but I'll still have those things that no one – no one – can ever take away.

And that's what we really want, isn't it? That's why we brag, that's why we work hard, that's why we get disappointed, that's why we fight, that's why we run away sometimes. We just want to love and be loved; we want to feel good about life, we want some peace of mind.

Let's ask God to give it to us. He did for me. Would you like to join me and lots of other old soldiers who have made the decision to quit trusting in our own weaknesses, and put our trust into the hands of Jesus Christ? Read this prayer to God – right now.

Father, I admit I've made mistakes in my life and continue to make them. I'm not qualified to enter heaven based on my own qualifications. I can fool other people, but You know that I'm just a schmuck. Thank You for sending Your son Jesus Christ to suffer the consequences of my screw-ups upon Himself. And based on Your promises in the Bible, I'm asking forgiveness for falling short, and for

You to take my life and make something good out of it. So, I'm now turning myself over to You, putting my trust in You. In Jesus' name. Amen

If this is your prayer, then I welcome you into the eternal brotherhood of the saints! Find a good church, if you don't have one already, and tell the pastor about the decision you made. And may God give you a life that exceeds any you may have expected on your own!

CPSIA information can be obtained
at www.ICGtesting.com
Printed in the USA
BVHW081348290121
598872BV00008B/1004